MW00885253

KINDNESS MAKES ME A SUPERHERO

Inspiring True Stories of Young Heroes Who Changed the World

MARTY HODGEF

TABLE OF CONTENTS

INTRODUCTION

Have you ever wished you could be a hero? What if you didn't need super strength, flying abilities, or even a cool costume? What if your superpower was something you already had inside—something simple, like kindness?

In these pages, you're going to meet kids who didn't wait around for magic to make a difference. They looked at the world around them and thought, How can I help? And guess what? Their kindness ended up creating real-life superpowers! From helping others to saving animals to protecting our planet, each story you'll read shows how just one person can spark amazing change.

You'll find stories of kids who started with small ideas—like collecting cans, sewing teddy bears, or planting a garden—that grew into powerful projects, bringing hope and joy to thousands of people. You'll even discover heroes who, from a young age, bravely stood up for causes they believed in, reminding everyone around them that kindness is a force that can't be stopped.

So, as you read, think about what your superpower could be. What matters to you? Where can you make a difference, big or small? These young heroes prove that kindness isn't just a nice thing to do; it's a powerful way to change the world. And who knows? Maybe you'll be the next story that inspires others.

Ready to find your own superpower? Let's jump into these stories and see where kindness can take us!

PART ONE

LOVE FOR ANIMALS CAN SAVE LIVES!

CHAPTER 1:

Saviors of Sea Turtles

Carter and Olivia Ries were just two animal-loving kids when they decided to make a big difference for endangered animals. One day, after learning about the threats facing creatures like sea turtles, they thought, Why shouldn't we help them out? And so, "One More Generation" was born. They had no idea it would turn into a huge movement to protect animals around the world—but they were ready to make it happen!

What made Carter and Olivia's mission even more special was that they didn't just talk about saving animals; they got their hands dirty, too! They rolled up their sleeves, grabbed some friends, and went out to the beaches, collecting trash and cleaning up places where endangered animals live. They were on a mission to make the world a safer place for sea turtles, pandas, rhinos—you name it! If it was endangered, Carter and Olivia wanted to help protect it.

But starting an organization isn't all fun and games. Carter and Olivia needed to tell people why it was so important to save animals, especially the ones that were in danger of disappearing forever. So, they visited schools, gave talks, and even spoke with government officials. People might not always think about sea turtles, elephants, or endangered frogs on a daily basis, but Carter and Olivia made it clear why we should all care. They showed that every little action counts and that if people joined in, they could make a massive difference for creatures all around the world.

One of the big problems they saw was all the plastic that ends up in the ocean. Sea turtles sometimes think floating plastic bags look like jellyfish (their favorite snack!), and if they eat them, it can make them really sick. Carter and Olivia decided to raise awareness about plastic pollution, launching cleanup projects with kids and adults. With gloves and bags in hand, they'd go out, pulling plastic off the beaches and out of rivers so animals wouldn't get hurt.

The siblings didn't stop there, though. They even created "Plastic Awareness Week" to get people everywhere to think about how much plastic they use and to try to cut it down. They encouraged families to try using reusable water bottles, to skip the plastic straws, and to bring their own bags when they go grocery shopping. Small changes, they knew, could add up if enough people got on board. It was all about doing one more thing to protect the planet—a perfect fit for their "One More Generation" movement.

When they were a bit older, Carter and Olivia got the chance to travel and meet conservationists (people who work to protect nature) from all over the world. They listened to stories about animals in places they'd only seen in books, like gorillas in Africa or snow leopards in the mountains. Each story inspired them to keep working, knowing that their efforts helped both animals close to home and those far away.

Their hard work didn't just help animals; it also inspired other kids to step up. They showed people everywhere that you don't have to be a scientist or grown-up to make a difference in the world. All you really need is passion, determination, and the belief that every little act of kindness counts. They wanted to protect "one more" species, inspire "one more" person, and make a lasting impact that would outlive them.

So, thanks to Carter and Olivia's endless energy, sea turtles have a cleaner, safer place to swim, and people are more aware of the dangers facing animals everywhere. These two siblings proved that kindness and care for the planet aren't just for grown-ups; they're for anyone willing to jump in, make a change, and leave a lasting legacy.

And who knows? Maybe you could be the next kid to help save a species or make a big impact. All it takes is an idea, a big heart, and the courage to take that first step—just like Carter and Olivia.

A LITTLE KINDNESS
BRINGS BIG SMILES!

CHAPTER 2:

The Teddy Bear Hero

Campbell Remess, or "Bumble" as he's known to friends and family, was just nine years old when he realized he wanted to make a difference. Living in Tasmania, Australia, Campbell had always had a big heart and an even bigger imagination. One day, he heard about kids in hospitals who felt lonely or scared, facing tough illnesses without much to cheer them up. Campbell thought to himself, What could I do to help? He didn't have much money to buy toys, but he had something even better—an idea and the determination to make it happen.

So, Campbell decided he would make his very own teddy bears to give to sick kids! He didn't know how to sew at first, but he was ready to learn. He asked his mom to teach him the basics, and soon, he was spending his afternoons surrounded by colorful fabrics, fluffy stuffing, and spools of thread. His goal was simple: to make one bear every day, no matter how long it took or how many stabs from the needle he got along the way.

Making a bear each day was no small challenge. Each teddy bear had to be carefully cut, stitched, and stuffed. Campbell wanted every bear to be just right, with a friendly face and soft arms perfect for hugs. He chose different colors and patterns, making each bear unique and special, just like the kids who would eventually receive them. Every time he finished a bear, he gave it a name and put it aside, ready for its new owner. Campbell thought about how each one might bring a smile to a child's face and help them feel braver.

Soon, Campbell's idea began to spread. People started calling him "the Teddy Bear Hero," and they wanted to know more about this boy who was making a difference with just a needle, thread, and a heart full of kindness. Campbell didn't just stop at his daily bear routine; he also started a project called "Project 365 by Campbell." His mission was to make 365 teddy bears each year, one for every single day. Friends, family, and even strangers loved his idea so much that they began sending him materials to keep up with his goal.

As Campbell's bears traveled to hospitals, children all over started receiving these special handmade gifts. For many kids, these bears became best friends they could hold onto when they felt scared or sad. Parents shared stories about how much these simple gifts meant to their children, and doctors noticed the positive impact the bears had on their young patients. Campbell was amazed by how much joy and comfort his bears could bring to others, even from something as simple as fabric and a bit of fluff.

Campbell didn't stop there. Every holiday season, he organized teddy bear drives, creating dozens of bears for special events and even reaching out to kids in need outside of the hospital. Over the years, Campbell has made hundreds of teddy bears, each one representing his dedication and kindness toward others. He's shared his story and inspired kids and adults alike to look for ways they can make a difference, no matter their age.

Campbell's teddy bear project is more than just about making toys. It's a symbol of how even a small act of kindness can grow into something big. With every bear, Campbell isn't just giving a gift—he's giving hope and comfort, showing sick kids that someone is thinking of them and cares about their happiness. His bears remind us all that no act of kindness is too small to make a difference, especially when it's from the heart.

Today, Campbell continues to make bears, spreading joy one stitch at a time and proving that kindness can come in all shapes and sizes—even as a soft, cuddly teddy bear made by a determined kid with a big heart.

EVERY KIND ACT BUILDS A BRIGHTER WORLD!

CHAPTER 3:

Building Kindness Brick by Brick

Rachel Wheeler was only 9 years old when she heard a story that would change her life—and the lives of many others, halfway around the world. She learned that in Haiti, a massive earthquake had left thousands of families homeless, without a safe place to sleep or even go to school. That hit Rachel hard. She couldn't stop thinking about how different her life was from those kids who didn't have a roof over their heads. But Rachel didn't just feel sorry for them—she felt fired up to help.

Rachel decided she was going to do something big, something that would really make a difference. She came up with a daring goal: to raise enough money to build homes for families who had lost everything. And we're not just talking about a little bit of money—Rachel set out to raise $250,000! That's right, a quarter of a million dollars, all from a 9-year-old girl with a huge heart.

So, how does a kid raise that much money? It started small. Rachel talked to her family, friends, neighbors, and pretty much anyone who would listen. She held bake sales, organized events and even went to businesses in her community, sharing her story and asking for support. She explained how she wanted to build homes where kids could feel safe and sleep soundly at night. Little by little, donations started pouring in. People were so inspired by Rachel's kindness and determination that they wanted to help her reach her goal.

As her fundraising picked up steam, Rachel realized something amazing: people wanted to be a part of her mission. They believed in her dream to build homes in Haiti because they could see how much it mattered to her. With every donation, Rachel got closer to her goal. And soon, that big number didn't seem so impossible anymore.

When Rachel reached the $250,000 mark, she was thrilled—but the real magic happened when she traveled to Haiti to see the homes she'd helped create. It wasn't just a pile of bricks; it was a neighborhood filled with families who now had a place to call home. Rachel had helped build 27 homes and even a school, creating a place where kids could learn, laugh, and grow up safely. These weren't just houses; they were a fresh start, a chance for families to rebuild their lives.

Rachel walked through the community she'd helped build and met some of the families.

She saw kids running around, playing games, and going to school, and she knew that her kindness had changed their lives. She wasn't just a girl from Florida anymore—she was someone who had made a difference in the lives of people she'd never even met.

But the best part? Rachel's kindness inspired others to start helping, too. Her story showed people that you don't have to be an adult or have tons of money to make a real difference. All you need is a big heart and the courage to take action. Rachel didn't have all the answers when she started; she just had the belief that everyone deserves a place to call home, no matter where they live.

By the time she was done, Rachel had proven that kindness is about more than just feeling sympathy—it's about doing something to help, even when the problem seems huge. She had seen a need, took action, and changed an entire community's future. And through her work, she reminded people everywhere that real kindness can move mountains (or, in her case, build homes).

Rachel Wheeler's story shows how a caring heart and determined mind can achieve incredible things. She turned her compassion into action, brick by brick, giving hope and new homes to those who needed them most.

SPEAK UP—NATURE NEEDS YOU!

CHAPTER 4:

A Voice for Nature

When Robbie Bond was just nine, he discovered something that shook him to his core: some of his favorite places in nature—the parks he loved to hike, play, and explore in—were under threat. U.S. national parks, those vast, beautiful landscapes filled with trees, rivers, mountains, and wildlife, were at risk of losing the protections that kept them safe from pollution and harm. Robbie knew that if something wasn't done, these parks might not be around for kids in the future to enjoy. And Robbie wasn't the kind of kid to just sit around and wait for someone else to fix things.

So, what did Robbie do? He got to work! He started his very own campaign called "Kids Speak for Parks." His mission was simple: get other kids like him to raise their voices and join the movement to protect national parks. Robbie believed that kids could make a big difference, and he was determined to prove it. He spoke out to show that national parks weren't just land—they were treasures, full of history, adventure, and natural beauty that belonged to everyone.

Robbie's campaign grew quickly, and soon, he was reaching out to schools, talking to classrooms, and encouraging other kids to get involved. He traveled all over, sharing his passion for nature and helping kids understand why national parks are so important. Robbie's message wasn't just about saving land; it was about saving a place where kids could experience nature, learn about wildlife, and feel a deep connection to the planet. He wanted everyone to understand that by protecting these places now, future generations would also get to enjoy them.

One of Robbie's favorite parts of "Kids Speak for Parks" was visiting national parks himself. He would hike the trails, snap photos, and share his experiences with other kids. He talked about the magic of standing in a forest surrounded by towering trees, seeing wild animals in their natural habitats, and feeling the peace that comes from simply being outside. Robbie wanted every kid to have a chance to feel the same way and learn to care about these parks as much as he did.

He also created a cool website and social media pages for his campaign, filled with facts about national parks, tips on how kids could get involved, and updates on events. He organized park cleanups, educational workshops, and even virtual events so kids from all over the country could participate.

Robbie's campaign was a huge success, and kids everywhere were excited to join him in protecting the places they loved.

Robbie's passion and kindness didn't just inspire kids; adults took notice, too. He met with leaders, gave interviews, and even spoke at events to spread his message as far as he could. When he talked, he didn't use big words or fancy explanations. He just spoke from the heart, sharing what the parks meant to him and why it was so important to keep them safe. People listened, and more and more kids signed up to be part of the "Kids Speak for Parks" movement.

Through his dedication, Robbie showed that kindness isn't just about helping people; it can also mean caring for the world around us. His efforts are a reminder that protecting nature is one of the most important ways we can show kindness—not just to the land but to each other and future generations. He taught kids everywhere that you don't have to be an adult to make a big difference; sometimes, a young voice can echo louder than anyone expected.

Today, Robbie continues to speak out, spreading his message about the importance of national parks and how each of us can play a part in protecting them. He's proof that when you care deeply about something, even a young person's actions can spark a movement that will help keep our world a little greener and a little kinder. Thanks to Robbie, kids everywhere are stepping up for nature and speaking out to protect the lands they love.

YOU CAN TURN ANYTHING INTO GOOD!

CHAPTER 5:

The Kid Who Turned Trash into Treasure

When Ryan Hickman was only three years old, he went on an adventure with his dad to the local recycling center. What was supposed to be a simple outing became a life-changing event for young Ryan. As he watched cans and bottles being sorted, crushed, and recycled, he realized something big—recycling could help protect the planet! He started thinking, "If recycling can make such a difference, why don't we do it all the time?"

After that day, Ryan couldn't stop talking about recycling. In fact, he was on a mission! He decided to start his very own recycling project, and he named it "Ryan's Recycling." Ryan's Recycling was no small deal. By the time he was seven, Ryan had already collected over 200,000 cans and bottles! He had raised thousands of dollars, and he was just getting started. His project wasn't just about collecting recyclables; it was about teaching everyone he knew about the importance of caring for the planet.

So how did Ryan do it? First, he set out on recycling adventures all around his neighborhood in California. Every time he saw a can or bottle lying around, he thought, "That's not trash; that's treasure!" He would gather up bags and bags of recyclables, sorting them with precision and making sure nothing went to waste. Soon, his friends and neighbors noticed his efforts, and before he knew it, people from all over were bringing their cans and bottles to him.

Ryan didn't just collect recyclables at home—he reached out to schools, local businesses, and even community events to share his love for recycling. He would show up with his famous big, blue recycling bins, ready to help others join the recycling movement. His enthusiasm was contagious. Adults started taking recycling more seriously, kids were excited to join in, and everyone wanted to be part of the change Ryan was creating.

What made Ryan's work extra special was that he wasn't just recycling for himself. The money he earned went toward environmental causes he believed in, like supporting marine animal rescue and organizations that worked to keep oceans clean. He knew that recycling didn't just help the planet on land—it also helped keep our oceans and rivers free from pollution, which meant happier sea animals like dolphins, turtles, and fish. Ryan's kindness didn't just help his neighborhood; it was making a difference around the world.

As Ryan's project grew, so did his fame. He was interviewed on TV shows, invited to speak at events, and became a recycling superstar! But no matter how famous he got, Ryan's goal never changed. He wanted to make recycling easy, fun, and something everyone could do. He continued to go to recycling centers, load up his bags with cans and bottles, and talk to people about why they should care for the planet, too. Ryan's Recycling was his way of showing kindness—not just to people but to the earth itself.

By now, Ryan has collected over a million cans and bottles, keeping a mountain of trash from ending up in landfills and oceans. He's shown that even the smallest action, like picking up a can or bottle, can have a big impact when enough people get involved. For

Ryan, it's not just about what he's done but also about what he's inspired others to do. His message is simple: everyone can make a difference, even if it starts with something as small as a soda can.

And that's how Ryan Hickman, a boy with a big heart and an even bigger recycling bag, turned trash into treasure, one can at a time. His kindness didn't come from just talking about saving the planet—it came from taking action, inspiring others, and showing that even one small choice can create big change for the world. Thanks to Ryan, more people are thinking about the planet, caring for their communities, and choosing to recycle with a smile.

MARTY HODGEF

PART TWO

HELPING OTHERS MAKES YOU A HERO!

CHAPTER 6:

A Champion for Childhood Cancer

Caleb Harper was just a regular 9-year-old with a big heart and a great group of friends. He loved hanging out, playing games, and doing everything kids his age enjoy. But one day, Caleb faced something that changed his world—he lost one of his close friends to cancer. For anyone, especially a kid, the loss of a friend feels unfair and hard to understand. But for Caleb, that sadness turned into something else, too—a powerful urge to help kids going through the same fight his friend had faced.

Caleb decided he couldn't just sit by. His friend's memory deserved more than that, and he wanted to make sure no one else would feel that same sadness if he could help it. So he came up with an idea: "What if I could raise money for pediatric cancer research and help kids who are still fighting this disease?" And that was how Caleb's fight Against Childhood Cancer was born.

Caleb wasn't just determined; he was creative, too. He organized bake sales, car washes, and even mini-sports events. Each event was packed with people who came out to support Caleb's cause, excited to be part of something important. He set up tables, helped bake treats, and did everything he could to make each fundraiser a success. Soon, people from his community, including friends, family, neighbors, and even people he didn't know, were donating to his cause. He showed everyone that even the smallest actions, when done with heart, could make a big difference.

And it didn't take long for Caleb's message to spread. More and more people heard about his mission, and he was suddenly the youngest person in his town to be leading a full-blown fundraising campaign! But Caleb didn't let the attention get to his head. He stayed focused on what mattered—helping kids with cancer and honoring his friend's memory. Every dollar he raised felt like a step toward a cure, and every event he held was a way to bring people together, spreading kindness through his commitment.

One of Caleb's biggest events was a community talent show he organized with the help of his friends and family. There were singers, dancers, magicians, and even a few funny skits that got everyone laughing. Not only was it a blast, but every single ticket sold went toward cancer research. Caleb watched as his community rallied together, bringing smiles and hope, not just for him but for families everywhere. Seeing people's excitement and generosity filled him with pride, knowing that each moment was one step closer to helping kids like his friend.

Caleb's campaign wasn't just about raising money; it was about inspiring others to get involved. He spoke at schools and events, sharing his story and encouraging kids to look out for one another. He explained that kindness wasn't just about being nice; it was about making choices to help others, even if they didn't ask for it. And Caleb practiced what he preached every day. His journey proved that any kid could step up and create change.

Over the years, Caleb's fight Against Childhood Cancer has continued to grow, reaching more and more people. His actions have inspired thousands, showing kids everywhere that age doesn't matter when it comes to making a difference. What mattered was the courage to act, to care, and to turn kindness into real, powerful action. And Caleb, with his unstoppable determination, had shown exactly how that was done.

Thanks to Caleb, people who had never met his friend now understood why fighting cancer was so important. He made it clear that kindness wasn't just about sympathy— it was about doing whatever you could, big or small, to make life a little better for those who need it most. And Caleb Harper, the kid with a mission, did exactly that.

ANYONE CAN MAKE A DIFFERENCE!

CHAPTER 7:

The Kid President

Once upon a time, in a world where kindness sometimes seemed lost among the chaos, a remarkable kid named Robbie Novak stepped onto the stage—well, more like the internet stage! At just 6 years old, he transformed into "Kid President," and with his charming smile and uplifting spirit, he set out on a mission to spread joy and compassion everywhere he went.

Robbie didn't just want to be any ordinary kid; he wanted to be the President of Kindness! He knew that being nice to others was one of the most powerful things anyone could do. After all, what's better than making someone's day a little brighter? With the help of his big brother and some creative ideas, Robbie created videos that quickly went viral, capturing the hearts of people around the globe.

In his videos, Robbie shared his funny yet wise thoughts on life. He wore a snazzy suit and tie, complete with a charming bow tie, and stood confidently in front of a backdrop that looked like the Oval Office. "What's up, everybody?" he would say, his voice brimming with excitement. "Let's talk about being awesome!" And then, in his own unique style, he would share his secrets for spreading kindness.

One of his most famous messages was simple yet powerful: "You should be nice to each other!" Robbie encouraged everyone to be their best selves and treat others with respect. He even had a "Secret to Being Awesome" list, which included things like giving compliments, sharing, and smiling. Who knew being kind could be so much fun?

But Robbie didn't stop there. He knew that actions speak louder than words, so he also teamed up with various charities and organizations to help those in need. He led campaigns to raise money for schools, food banks, and even animal shelters. For him, kindness wasn't just a catchphrase; it was a way of life!

One of his most touching projects was during the holiday season when Robbie created a movement called "The Best Holiday Ever." He encouraged kids to think of others instead of just themselves. He asked everyone to give away their old toys and clothes to those who needed them more. Robbie's enthusiasm was contagious, and soon, kids all around the country were joining in, creating a ripple effect of giving!

As Robbie's popularity grew, so did his platform. He was invited to speak at various events, where he inspired even more people to spread kindness. Imagine a kid standing in front of hundreds of adults, confidently sharing how important it is to treat everyone with love and respect. That was Robbie! He made kindness cool, and soon, people began to realize that making a difference could start right at home.

But what made Robbie's story truly special was his ability to connect with everyone. He understood that kindness didn't have to be a grand gesture; it could be as simple as holding the door open for someone or sharing a smile. He encouraged kids to be leaders in their schools and communities, reminding them that even though they were young, their voices mattered.

One day, during a school visit, Robbie told the kids, "You are never too little to make a difference! If I can do it, so can you!" Those words ignited a spark in everyone's hearts. Kids started their own kindness clubs, organized toy drives, and even volunteered at local shelters—all because Robbie inspired them to take action.

As Robbie continued to create more videos, his messages reached millions of people. He shared stories of everyday heroes, highlighting those who went out of their way to help others. Through his eyes, the world became a better place, one kind act at a time.

Robbie Novak, the Kid President, showed us all that kindness can change the world. It doesn't take a superhero cape or magical powers; all it takes is a caring heart and the courage to act. His journey reminds us that no matter how young we are, we can all be champions of kindness, spreading joy wherever we go!

SMALL GIFTS BRING BIG JOY!

CHAPTER 8:

Spreading Kindness, One Kit at a Time

Cavanaugh Bell might just be one of the youngest kindness warriors you've ever heard of! At only seven years old, he started a movement to spread positivity, fight against bullying, and make the world a friendlier place for everyone. And with his big heart and unstoppable spirit, he has done just that.

It all began because of something no one should ever have to go through: bullying. Cavanaugh experienced the harsh words and actions of kids who weren't treating him kindly, and it hurt deeply. But instead of letting it break him down, he decided to take a stand—not just for himself, but for others too. He wanted everyone to feel safe, happy, and respected, so he came up with an idea to make his community a better place.

Cavanaugh was determined to spread kindness far and wide, and his first mission was to create something he called "Kindness Kits." What exactly is a Kindness Kit? Well, each one is filled with essential items—like socks, toiletries, snacks, and other things that people experiencing homelessness might need. His goal was simple: to help others feel cared for and show them that someone out there was rooting for them.

Cavanaugh started raising money to put together these Kindness Kits. He didn't have piles of money to begin with, but he wasn't going to let that stop him. He asked for donations, held small fundraisers, and spread the word about his mission. Soon, people were inspired by his kindness and jumped in to help. He collected enough donations to fill hundreds of kits! With each one he packed, he thought about the person who would receive it, hoping they'd feel seen and valued.

When it came time to deliver the kits, Cavanaugh was ready. Alongside his family, he handed out these Kindness Kits at homeless shelters and to people in need. The smiles he received in return filled his heart with joy. And he quickly learned that kindness wasn't just about the gifts he gave—it was about letting people know they mattered.

But Cavanaugh wasn't done yet. Once he started, he realized there was so much more he could do. He organized "community days," where he invited people to come together to pack even more kits, collect food donations, and volunteer in their neighborhoods.

Cavanaugh believed that if everyone took just a little bit of time to help others, the world would be an amazing place.

Word of Cavanaugh's kindness spread fast, and people from all over began to take notice. He even had the chance to meet with local leaders and speak about his experiences with bullying and the power of kindness. He encouraged them to make changes that would help kids feel safer at school and supported in their communities. Through it all, Cavanaugh stood proud, showing that kindness is strong and can make waves that reach far and wide.

Cavanaugh's story is proof that no one is too young to make a difference. His heart, as big as it is, continues to grow as he helps more and more people. He's worked on projects to deliver food to families in need, especially during hard times when many people needed extra help. In total, he's helped deliver thousands of pounds of food and hundreds of Kindness Kits and brought smiles to countless faces.

Today, Cavanaugh keeps inspiring other kids to step up and join the kindness movement. He encourages everyone to find their own ways to help, no matter how big or small. Whether it's helping a neighbor, standing up for someone who's being picked on, or simply sharing a kind word, Cavanaugh believes each little act can make a huge difference. And you know what? He's absolutely right.

So, let Cavanaugh's journey motivate you to take action. There's always something kind we can do, whether for a friend, a family member, or even a stranger. Because in a world where kindness spreads from one person to the next, everyone has the chance to feel valued. And just like Cavanaugh, you can be a hero of kindness, too!

CHAPTER 9:

The Fighter for Freedom

Sophie Cruz was just five years old when she discovered that something big, something really important, was happening around her. Her parents, who had moved to the United States from Mexico, were worried about their future in a country that wasn't their birthplace. Even though she was just a little kid, Sophie could see that something was making her family afraid—and she decided she wasn't going to stand by and do nothing. She wanted to help.

Now, you might think, "What can a five-year-old do in a situation that even grown-ups are struggling with?" But Sophie didn't let that stop her. She was determined to speak up, not just for her parents, but for thousands of families who faced the same worry and fear. She believed that families should be able to stay together and that everyone deserved kindness, respect, and safety, no matter where they were from.

So what did Sophie do? She wrote a letter. Not just any letter, either—she wrote a heartfelt letter to the President of the United States! Sophie knew that the President had the power to make changes, and she hoped that her words, even though they came from a five-year-old, would make a difference. With the help of her family and community, she made her way to Washington, D.C., to deliver that letter, filled with hope and bravery, straight to the leader of the country.

When Sophie arrived, she didn't go unnoticed. In fact, people were amazed to

KINDNESS MAKES ME A SUPERHERO

see someone so young with such a huge, important message. And Sophie didn't stop there. She continued to speak up in big ways—at rallies, in interviews, and even on stage at events where thousands of people gathered. Sophie's voice was small, but her message was loud and clear: kindness, courage, and love for one's family were values everyone should stand up for.

At one rally, Sophie wore a bright yellow dress and a huge smile as she spoke to the crowd. She held her head high, even though the microphone almost seemed too big for her. Her words were simple yet powerful. She told the crowd, "We are children, we are loved, and we deserve to be with our families." The crowd cheered and clapped. Sophie's bravery showed people everywhere that kindness means caring about others, even if it feels a little scary at times.

But that wasn't all Sophie did. She became an advocate for immigrant rights, which is a big way of saying she spoke out to protect people who were worried about being separated from their families or their homes. Sophie went on to become a symbol of hope and bravery for people all over the country. People who felt alone, scared, or overlooked looked up to Sophie, realizing that if this young girl could be brave, they could too.

Sophie's courage didn't only inspire other kids—her actions inspired adults as well! She reminded everyone that kindness can be as simple as standing up for what you believe in, even if you're the youngest person in the room. And Sophie never backed down. She continued to travel, give speeches, and show everyone that kindness can be a powerful force for good, especially when it's driven by a passion to help others.

Through all her speeches, marches, and interviews, Sophie taught people that being brave isn't just about feeling fearless. Real bravery is caring enough to take action even when it feels difficult or uncertain. Her kindness came from a deep place of love and loyalty to her family and to families everywhere. She showed the world that kindness and courage go hand in hand, no matter how young you are.

Thanks to Sophie, thousands of people have a reason to feel hopeful, loved, and supported. She proved that one voice, even a small one, could make a big difference. When we care about something enough to stand up for it, just like Sophie, we have the power to bring kindness and hope to those who need it most. And sometimes, that's all it takes to make the world a better place.

GROW KINDNESS—IT
BLOOMS EVERYWHERE!

CHAPTER 10:

Growing Goodness in the Garden

At just ten years old, Ian McKenna found a way to make a difference right in his own backyard. When he learned that some kids in his community didn't have enough to eat, he wanted to do something about it. But he didn't just stop at giving snacks or canned food. Ian came up with a unique idea that combined his love for the outdoors with his desire to help others: he would start a garden to grow fresh vegetables and fruits and give them away to families in need.

Ian's project began small, but it was packed with big dreams. He named it Ian's Giving Garden, and it became his mission to grow food for those who needed it. With a few seeds, some tools, and a whole lot of heart, he started planting rows of vegetables right in his backyard. Soon, he had tomatoes, cucumbers, peppers, and even watermelons sprouting up, and every single plant had one purpose—to help others.

Gardening wasn't as easy as it looked, though. Ian had to learn a lot about soil, watering, and keeping pests away from his plants. But he never gave up. He got up early to water his plants before school, pulled weeds on weekends, and even braved some of the hottest summer days to keep his garden healthy. And when it came time to harvest, Ian didn't just fill up his own plate; he shared his bounty with families who needed it most.

Word spread fast about Ian's garden, and soon, his friends, neighbors, and even his classmates wanted to get involved. Some kids helped him plant new seeds, while others pitched in to pull weeds or water the crops. Ian made it clear that this garden wasn't just his—it was a community garden, and everyone could be a part of the project to help others.

Ian also loved teaching kids his age about gardening. He showed them how to carefully plant seeds, how to pick ripe vegetables, and the right way to water without overdoing it. Before long, Ian's Giving Garden was not only feeding families, but it was also inspiring other kids to start growing their own gardens or volunteering in their communities.

As the garden grew, so did Ian's dreams. He started building more garden beds and planting even more kinds of fruits and veggies. He added lettuce, carrots, strawberries, and herbs, making sure that his Giving Garden provided a variety of healthy foods. He even started composting, turning kitchen scraps into rich soil to help his plants grow strong.

Ian's project became a great example of how kindness and caring for others could lead to something truly amazing. With every tomato, pepper, and cucumber he harvested, Ian was spreading kindness and showing that no one was too young to make a big difference. Ian's Giving Garden became a lifeline for people who needed fresh food, and it was proof that a simple idea, like planting seeds, could grow into something powerful.

Over the years, Ian's Giving Garden has grown from a small backyard plot to a full community effort. People come together to help him plant, water, and harvest, all working toward a common goal of helping those in need. Thanks to Ian's determination and kindness, many families have access to fresh produce that they otherwise might not have had. And every time Ian sees the smiles on their faces, he knows that all the hard work is worth it.

Through his Giving Garden, Ian taught his community a valuable lesson: kindness is something that grows. Just like the plants in his garden, kindness starts small but can flourish into something incredible when given the right care. With his Giving Garden, Ian didn't just feed people's bodies—he fed their hearts, too, showing that anyone with a bit of soil, some seeds, and a caring heart can create something that nourishes a whole community.

PART THREE

CHANGE MAKERS IN ACTION

KINDNESS IS FOR
EVERYONE!

CHAPTER 11:

Creating a World of Access and Kindness

When Alex Knoll was twelve, he noticed something most people never even think about. He saw that people with disabilities—those who use wheelchairs, have vision impairments, or need other special accommodations—often have a hard time finding accessible places in their communities. Whether it's a restaurant without a ramp, a movie theater with no hearing assistance, or a park with paths that aren't easy to get around, there are so many things that can make life more challenging for people with disabilities.

But while most people would just shrug and move on, Alex didn't. He thought, Why not do something to help? Alex wanted to make the world more inclusive—a place where everyone, no matter their abilities, could feel welcome and find the things they needed. That's when he got a big idea: an app that could help people find accessible spots in their area right from their phones. And so, the "Ability App" was born!

Creating an app might sound like a job for a grown-up or a team of tech experts, but Alex didn't let his age hold him back. He was only twelve, but he had a vision and enough kindness to fill a thousand apps. Alex got to work researching, designing, and reaching out for support. He wanted the app to include all kinds of information, from which places had wheelchair ramps to which restaurants had menus in Braille. He imagined an app where people could search for places that fit their needs without worrying about what obstacles they might face.

Alex's parents saw how passionate he was and encouraged him, but it was still a lot of work. He spent hours reading about accessibility issues, talking to people with disabilities, and learning how apps are built. He even spoke with experts in the field to make sure he was getting it right. Alex was determined to make the Ability App as helpful as possible, and he wasn't going to stop until he did.

Word about Alex's project spread quickly. Soon, newspapers and TV shows were reaching out to interview him. Alex was nervous at first but soon realized that sharing his vision with others could inspire them to help, too. He explained his idea to large audiences, reminding them that small things—like a ramp, a wider door, or a Braille sign—could make a huge difference in someone's life.

It wasn't long before his story caught the attention of some pretty big names in the tech world. He even got invited to visit tech companies and meet professionals who encouraged him to keep working on his dream. They admired how someone so young was already making such a big impact. Alex didn't let the attention distract him; he just kept working to improve the Ability App, adding features and expanding its reach so that more people could use it.

The most amazing thing about Alex's journey was how much kindness and thoughtfulness he put into every step. He wasn't creating the app for fame or money. He was doing it because he genuinely cared about making the world a better place. He wanted people to feel comfortable and welcome wherever they went without having to worry about whether or not a place could meet their needs. His kindness was his superpower, and it helped him to build something truly life-changing.

Today, the Ability App continues to grow, helping people with disabilities navigate their communities with greater ease. Alex's creation makes it easier for people to go out, try new places, and enjoy their neighborhoods without barriers holding them back. His work has made a real difference in so many people's lives, giving them more freedom to explore, connect, and enjoy the world.

Alex showed everyone that kindness doesn't have to be complicated. Sometimes, it's as simple as noticing a problem and deciding to help. His story is a perfect example of how one person's caring heart can bring joy, comfort, and freedom to others in ways they might never expect.

Thanks to Alex, more people can confidently go wherever they want to go—and his kindness continues to inspire others to create a world where everyone belongs.

KINDNESS MAKES ME A SUPERHERO

EVERY KIND STEP COUNTS!

CHAPTER 12:

Racing to Kindness

Orion Jean was only 10 years old when he decided it was time to get into the game. Not a video game or a soccer game, but a race— a race for kindness. It all started during the COVID-19 pandemic when the world felt upside-down, and Orion noticed that lots of people were struggling. So, he set out to do something about it.

Orion called his mission the "Race to Kindness." And boy, did he take that name seriously! Like a runner on the starting line, he was ready to move fast and bring kindness wherever he went. But instead of medals and trophies, his race was all about helping as many people as possible. And he didn't need superpowers or magical gadgets—just a big heart and some determination.

The first leg of Orion's "Race to Kindness" began with a toy drive. Orion knew that toys could make kids smile, especially during tough times when they might feel scared or lonely. So, he set a goal to collect 500 toys for children in need. He talked to family, friends, and even people he didn't know, sharing his goal and explaining why it mattered. Soon, the toys started rolling in like waves, and Orion not only met his goal but went above and beyond it!

With his toy drive a success, Orion didn't slow down. He was just getting started! For the next part of his mission, he decided to provide meals to those who were hungry. Orion was shocked to learn that millions of people around the world, including many families in his own community, didn't have enough food to eat. So, he kicked off a "Race to 100,000 Meals" campaign. That's right—100,000 meals! It sounded like an impossible number, but to Orion, it was a challenge worth taking.

He got to work, contacting local businesses, food banks, and restaurants. Every time he reached a small goal, he just kept pushing forward, like a marathon runner going mile after mile. Orion's family and community rallied around him, donating, volunteering, and spreading the word. Before he knew it, Orion's "Race to Kindness" provided thousands of meals to people in need, filling their bellies and lifting their spirits.

But Orion's race wasn't over yet. For the next stretch, he decided to focus on something close to his heart—books! He knew that books were more than just pages with words; they were adventures, lessons, and new worlds to explore. He wanted every kid to have access to books, no matter where they came from. So, he launched a campaign to collect and donate 500,000 books to kids across the country.

Once again, Orion worked tirelessly, reaching out to schools, libraries, and publishers. The books started piling up in towers around him, each one destined for a young reader. With each book he gave, Orion was sharing the gift of knowledge, imagination, and hope.

Through it all, Orion's message was simple but powerful: kindness isn't a one-time thing; it's something you can keep doing again and again. He didn't want kids to just hear about his story; he wanted them to join him. Orion's "Race to Kindness" became an invitation, a call for kids everywhere to find their own ways to help others. It didn't have to be as big as donating thousands of meals or toys. To Orion, every small act of kindness was part of the race, whether it was holding a door open, sharing a snack, or simply being a good friend.

Orion proved that one person—even a kid—can start a movement. By donating toys, meals, and books, he showed that kindness can be powerful enough to make a difference in the lives of many. In doing so, he inspired other kids to think about how they could spread kindness, too.

Orion's 'Race to Kindness' may have started with one big heart, but it's grown into something even bigger, with kids all over joining in. His story shows that kindness isn't a race you win; it's one that never ends.

HEALTHY CHOICES HELP EVERYONE!

CHAPTER 13:

Bringing Health to the Table

When Haile Thomas was only twelve, something happened in her family that changed the way she looked at food. Her dad was diagnosed with diabetes, a condition that meant he had to be very careful about what he ate and how he took care of his body. Haile was worried but determined to help, so she dove headfirst into learning everything she could about healthy eating. She discovered that the food choices we make can have a huge impact on our health and happiness.

But Haile didn't stop there. She started thinking about how many other kids might not know just how powerful good nutrition could be, especially if it could help them avoid health problems like her dad was facing. She realized that eating well didn't have to be boring or taste bad; it could actually be fun and delicious! So, instead of just keeping her knowledge to herself, Haile decided to share it with kids everywhere. That's when she created The HAPPY Organization.

The HAPPY Organization stands for Healthy, Active, Positive Purposeful Youth, and Haile had one main goal: to make learning about healthy eating exciting. She wanted to show that fruits and vegetables could be colorful, tasty, and just as fun as candy or chips. Haile's mission wasn't just about teaching kids facts; it was about inspiring them to make choices that would make them feel awesome, inside and out.

Haile started holding workshops, giving cooking demos, and talking to kids about healthy choices in a way that actually made sense. She didn't just throw around big, fancy words; she explained things simply and with lots of energy. Haile taught kids how to make cool snacks like rainbow salads and smoothies, showing them that a little creativity could make healthy food taste even better than junk food. And she didn't just talk about nutrition—she helped kids get hands-on in the kitchen, mixing, chopping, and learning how to make easy meals they could share with their families.

Pretty soon, her work was making waves. News outlets wanted to interview her, schools invited her to speak, and kids were getting excited about healthy eating in a way they never had before. Haile even got to meet some famous chefs and health experts who admired her commitment to helping kids live their best, healthiest lives.

One of the coolest things about Haile's journey is how she made healthy eating a family affair. She encouraged kids to get their parents, brothers, sisters, and even grandparents involved. She'd tell them, "Cooking together is fun, and it's a great way to make memories with the people you love!" Her kindness extended beyond just teaching; she truly cared about making sure families felt empowered to eat well and live well together.

Over time, Haile's organization grew, reaching kids across the country. She started sharing recipes and tips online so kids who couldn't meet her in person could still learn from her. Haile's message was simple: making healthy choices was a way to show kindness to yourself and the people around you. By taking care of your body, you were getting ready to do amazing things in the world. Her work helped so many kids realize that they had the power to choose foods that made them feel strong, energetic, and ready to tackle any challenge.

Haile's story is about more than just food; it's about kindness, courage, and the power of sharing what you know to help others. She proved that one kid with a caring heart could make a big difference, teaching others the importance of health in a way that was inspiring and easy to understand.

Thanks to Haile, kids all over are not just eating healthier—they're building stronger, more joyful lives. Her kindness is helping create a world where young people grow up knowing that they can take care of themselves and others with every delicious, healthy choice they make.

YOUR ACTIONS CAN BRING HOPE!

CHAPTER 14:

The Boy Who Built a Well for the World

Ryan Hreljac was just an ordinary six-year-old kid with a big smile, a love for soccer, and lots of energy. But one day, something happened that would make him anything but ordinary. It all started in his first-grade class, where Ryan's teacher began explaining how people in some parts of the world don't have clean water to drink, cook with, or even wash their hands. Ryan was a little surprised – how could people live without something as basic as water?

Ryan's teacher explained how far kids in some countries, especially in parts of Africa, have to walk every day just to find a muddy pond to get water. And even that water wasn't safe to drink! Sometimes, kids would get sick, but they didn't have a choice. Ryan listened with wide eyes, shocked and sad. He couldn't believe that something he'd always taken for granted was so rare and precious to others.

On his way home, Ryan's thoughts raced. He wondered if there was a way he could help these kids so they could have clean water, too. That night, he asked his mom and dad, "How much does it cost to build a well?" They chuckled at first, thinking it was just one of those questions kids ask. But Ryan wasn't joking. He wanted to know.

So, his parents did some research. The answer? Seventy dollars – just to start. For a six-year-old, seventy dollars sounded like a fortune, but Ryan was determined. He was going to raise every dollar of it, no matter how long it took.

At first, Ryan did extra chores around the house. He cleaned his room without being asked, helped with the dishes, and even pulled weeds in the garden. He saved every dollar and every penny until he finally had seventy dollars. With a proud smile, he handed the money over, ready to make his well a reality.

But then he got another surprise. The real cost of a well was actually closer to two thousand dollars, much more than his first seventy! This could have discouraged anyone, especially a first-grader, but Ryan didn't give up. Instead, he set his sights even higher, determined to raise the full amount.

Word about Ryan's mission spread around his school, then through his town, and eventually, people from far and wide heard about the little boy with a big heart.

Donations started pouring in, and people offered to help. Ryan's friends pitched in, and his family encouraged him. Soon enough, he'd raised not just two thousand dollars but enough for a well to be dug in Uganda, a country far away from his home in Canada.

When Ryan saw pictures of the well and the happy faces of the kids who could now drink clean water, he knew he couldn't stop at just one. He had seen the difference his kindness could make, and he wanted to do more. So, with the help of his family, Ryan started the "Ryan's Well Foundation." This way, he could keep helping other kids get access to clean water.

Ryan's kindness didn't just help one village – his foundation has helped thousands of communities and provided clean water to over a million people. All because one little boy saw a need and decided to act on it.

Today, Ryan's story has inspired countless other kids and grown-ups to think about how they can make a difference, too. Ryan learned that kindness sometimes means noticing a problem, no matter how big, and doing what you can to solve it. And sometimes, it means helping people you may never meet halfway across the world.

SPEAK FOR THE EARTH—
IT'S LISTENING!

CHAPTER 15:

Speaking Up for the Planet

At 15 years old, Greta Thunberg wasn't the type of kid who sat back quietly. Living in Sweden, she loved the forests, the crisp snow, and the clean lakes. But when she learned about climate change, Greta felt something shift in her heart. The earth, with its clean air and wild spaces, was in trouble. Scientists warned that humans were using too many natural resources, burning too many fossil fuels, and creating too much pollution. All this was leading to rising temperatures, melting glaciers, and stronger storms. Greta felt the need to speak up.

Most kids might have gone on with their day after learning about something so huge. But Greta was different. She kept thinking, Why aren't the grown-ups doing something about this? She knew that every year wasted was like losing precious time to help the planet. So, she decided to take matters into her own hands.

One morning, Greta put together a simple but bold plan: she would skip school and sit outside the Swedish parliament building with a sign. In big letters, her sign read, "School Strike for Climate." She wanted the leaders of her country to see her and realize how important climate action was. She didn't think it would change the world; she was just one kid trying to do her part.

On that first day, Greta sat alone. People passed by, some taking a curious look at the quiet girl with the determined face and hand-painted sign. A few people even stopped to ask why she wasn't in school. Greta explained patiently that she was skipping class to raise awareness about climate change because if adults weren't listening, she would make them listen.

Day after day, Greta returned to her spot, rain or shine. Soon, she started to get noticed by reporters, who were curious about this brave young girl. Word spread and kids all over the world started thinking, If Greta can do it, maybe I can too. They began organizing their own climate strikes, holding signs and sharing Greta's message of urgency for protecting the earth.

Before long, Greta's simple school strike became a global movement. Thousands of kids, teenagers, and even some adults joined in. They wanted their leaders to pay attention to the future of the planet and to make choices that would protect it. Greta began giving speeches, traveling to different countries to share her message, always with the same calm determination. Her speeches weren't fancy or filled with big words – they were honest and straightforward. She spoke from the heart, and people listened.

One of the most powerful moments came when she stood before world leaders at the United Nations. She looked them in the eye and said, "How dare you!" She was disappointed in the leaders for not doing enough to protect the environment and the future of kids like her. Greta's voice was small, but her words were big and powerful.

Greta's message wasn't just about fighting climate change. It was also about kindness – not just to other people but to animals, forests, oceans, and the entire planet. Her strike taught everyone that kindness can look different than we expect. It might be as simple as picking up litter in your park, recycling, or biking instead of driving. But sometimes, it's about speaking up for what's right, even if it feels hard or scary.

Thanks to Greta, millions of people are now more aware of climate change. Kids everywhere know they have the power to make a difference, even if they're young. Greta showed them that caring about the planet is an act of kindness that helps everyone – today and in the future.

Her message lives on in classrooms, communities, and families around the world, showing that standing up for the earth can be one of the greatest acts of kindness. Greta's story isn't just about a school strike; it's about choosing to care, speak up, and make a positive change for everyone.

MARTY HODGEF

PART FOUR

DREAMS OF A BETTER WORLD

ONE IDEA CAN CHANGE
THE WORLD!

CHAPTER 16:

The Girl Who Sparked a Movement

At just eight years old, Hannah Taylor did something extraordinary. One winter day, she was out with her mom when she saw something that stopped her in her tracks—a man, cold and shivering, searching through a garbage bin for food. Hannah had never seen someone so desperate for a meal before, and it struck her hard. She felt a wave of sadness, confusion, and compassion all at once. At that moment, little Hannah knew she wanted to do something to help people like him, people who had nowhere to go and nothing to eat.

After they returned home, Hannah kept thinking about that man. She couldn't shake the image from her mind. At dinner, she turned to her mom and asked, "Why would someone have to eat from a garbage can?" Her mom explained that some people didn't have homes, and not everyone could afford food. Hannah was shocked. How could people live like that while others had warm beds, clothes, and plenty to eat?

Hannah's mind was buzzing with questions and ideas. Soon enough, she decided she was going to do something about it. She had a mission, and nothing was going to stop her. She shared her thoughts with her parents and friends, and they encouraged her to follow her heart. So, with a mixture of determination, kindness, and creativity, Hannah took her first steps toward helping those in need.

Her plan started small. Hannah began by collecting loose change and donations from her friends and neighbors. At school, she gave a talk to her classmates about what she had seen and why she felt it was important to help. Her classmates were so moved by her speech that they wanted to join her. Hannah's friends began donating their allowances, collecting coins from their family members, and even baking cookies to raise money. Slowly, more and more people heard about Hannah's efforts, and her mission began to grow.

Hannah didn't stop there. Soon, she came up with an idea to create an organization. But what should she call it? After a lot of thought, she decided on "The Ladybug Foundation." Why ladybugs? To Hannah, ladybugs symbolize good luck, protection, and hope. She thought of them as tiny little heroes, spreading kindness and helping wherever they could. Through the Ladybug

Foundation, Hannah wanted to be like a ladybug, helping people who needed it most.

Over the next few years, Hannah's foundation grew bigger than she could have ever imagined. What started as a small idea turned into a powerful movement. People from her community, and eventually all over Canada, started donating money, food, clothing, and supplies. Hannah used these resources to support homeless shelters and programs that helped people living in poverty. Her foundation provided meals, warm clothing, beds, and much-needed supplies to people who had little to nothing. Her goal was to give everyone the dignity and comfort they deserved.

As she got older, Hannah became a true advocate for homeless people. She met with government leaders, giving speeches about the importance of compassion and the need for better support for those without homes. She spoke with such passion that people couldn't help but listen. She even managed to inspire politicians to take action, putting policies in place to support homeless programs across the country.

Hannah's story powerfully shows that you're never too young to make a difference. She saw something that bothered her and decided not to look away. Instead, she took action and inspired thousands of others to do the same. Through her efforts, Hannah helped change the lives of countless people, providing warmth, food, and hope to those who needed it most.

With her Ladybug Foundation, Hannah Taylor showed the world that kindness and compassion could make a real impact. Whether you're eight, eighteen, or eighty, you have the power to change lives by caring about others and taking action.

SHARING FOOD IS
SHARING LOVE!

CHAPTER 17:

The Boy Who Brought Food to Those in Need

Aidan Riley was only 13 when he noticed a big problem during the COVID-19 pandemic. While so many people were going hungry, tons of food were going to waste on farms. He was shocked to learn that, across the country, farmers were being forced to let perfectly good produce rot because they couldn't sell or distribute it. Grocery stores were closed or had limited stock, and people were struggling to find food at a time when everyone needed it most. Aidan thought,

"Why can't we get this extra food to people who really need it?"

Most 13-year-olds would have stopped there, maybe even written a school paper on the issue. But Aidan had a different idea: he wanted to make a real change, and he wasn't going to wait for someone else to do it. He called up a friend, and together, they came up with a bold plan to connect farms with food banks directly. And with that, the FarmLink Project was born.

The first step was reaching out to farmers. Aidan knew that the farmers had too much food on their hands, but they didn't have the right trucks, storage, or even the staff to get it to food banks. Aidan and his friend started making phone calls to local farms, introducing themselves, and explaining what they wanted to do. At first, some farmers were surprised to hear from a couple of teenagers! But once Aidan explained his plan, they were thrilled to help. They wanted their food to reach people, not go to waste.

Next, Aidan needed to find food banks that could take in the extra food. With even more calls and emails, he started to connect with food banks in his area. Food banks were also thrilled—suddenly, they had an option to get fresh fruits, vegetables, and other foods that were usually hard to come by. For them, Aidan's plan was a huge blessing.

But there was one more big problem to solve: transportation. Getting food from farms to food banks wasn't as simple as tossing it in a car. They needed big trucks and volunteers who could drive them. Aidan and his team worked tirelessly, contacting transportation companies, volunteers, and even trucking schools to see if anyone could help them out. Eventually, people started to pitch in. They found trucking companies and even raised money for the gas and rental trucks needed to get the project rolling.

As FarmLink grew, Aidan got even more people involved. His friends joined in, volunteering to make calls and help with logistics. They built a team of dedicated young people, all working together to make sure food didn't go to waste. Soon, the FarmLink Project was connecting hundreds of farms and food banks, reaching people who desperately needed fresh food.

It wasn't always easy. Aidan and his team faced setbacks—some days, transportation fell through, or food banks were overstocked and couldn't take more deliveries. But no matter what, Aidan kept pushing forward. He didn't let problems stop him. He knew that for every load of food they managed to deliver, families were getting fresh, nutritious meals that they might not have had otherwise.

As the months went by, FarmLink turned into a powerful movement. Aidan's small idea became a nationwide effort, with people all across the country hearing about the project and joining in to help. Volunteers from different states pitched in, and other teenagers got inspired by Aidan's determination and kindness. They saw how a simple idea could make a huge difference, and suddenly, FarmLink was rescuing millions of pounds of food that would have been wasted.

Thanks to Aidan's vision and commitment, millions of meals have been provided to people who needed them, while tons of food was saved from rotting away on farms. Aidan showed that sometimes kindness means rolling up your sleeves and doing something, even if it's hard work. He showed that, no matter how young you are, you can make a massive difference if you care enough to act. His work wasn't just about feeding people; it was about inspiring everyone around him to look for ways they could help, too.

The FarmLink Project continues to grow and help people across the country. And it all started with one teenager who saw a problem, took action, and inspired countless others to do the same.

YOU HAVE THE POWER TO
BRING JOY!

CHAPTER 18:

The Girl Who Made Wishes Come True

Ruby Kate Chitsey might sound like an ordinary kid, but what she did for people in nursing homes was nothing short of magical. At only 11 years old, Ruby noticed something that most people her age (or even much older) often miss: the small, everyday wishes of people who live in nursing homes. And it wasn't about big stuff like fancy trips or expensive gadgets—it was the simple things, like comfy shoes, snacks, or a cuddle with a furry friend, that the residents hoped for.

It all started when Ruby Kate visited a nursing home with her mom, who worked there as a nurse. While her mom was busy, Ruby went around chatting with the residents, asking about their lives, their memories, and even their favorite snacks. As she got to know them, Ruby realized many residents felt a little lonely and wished for small things that made them happy. For example, one lady missed her dog so much that it was like a big hole in her heart. Another man wished for some decent socks because his socks were worn out. Ruby felt a spark light up inside her—what if she could grant these little wishes?

Ruby thought to herself, "Why shouldn't I try to help?" But where would an 11-year-old get the money to buy all these things? After all, this wasn't like saving up for a toy or a game; this was going to help tons of people! So Ruby took action in a way that anyone could: she set up a fundraiser, sharing her idea with friends, family, and eventually, anyone who would listen. Soon enough, people were pitching in! With every dollar she raised, Ruby turned those dollars into something meaningful for the nursing home residents. She bought snacks, slippers, and soft blankets and even brought in pets to visit people who missed their own.

She called her project "Three Wishes for Ruby's Residents." The goal? To make sure every person she met could have at least three things they wished for. As she kept going, more and more people wanted to help, and her project grew into a full-blown organization. Ruby wasn't just buying random things—she was taking the time to really listen to each person's story, learning what mattered most to them. For some, it was a specific treat from their childhood. For others, it was a small item that held big memories.

Ruby saw how one small act could make someone's day so much brighter. She learned that kindness doesn't always need to be something huge. It can be a soft sweater for someone who feels cold or a few coloring books for someone who loves to draw. It can be as simple as a cup of tea, just the way someone likes it.

The residents of the nursing home began looking forward to Ruby's visits. Her kindness gave them something to look forward to, and her actions inspired people all over the country. Ruby even got to speak about her project on TV, and soon, "Three Wishes for Ruby's Residents" became a big name in kindness.

By caring enough to ask people what they wanted, Ruby found a way to make their lives a little warmer, brighter, and happier. And though she started small, her heart was big enough to create change that spread far beyond her town.

KINDNESS MAKES ME A SUPERHERO

CARING FOR ANIMALS IS KINDNESS!

CHAPTER 19:

The Young Advocate with a Heart for Animals

At 12 years old, Thomas Ponce didn't have the usual hobby like skateboarding or video games. Instead, he was busy working to make the world a safer, kinder place—for animals. Thomas had always loved animals, but when he learned that some animals were treated unfairly or harmed, it made his heart ache. Instead of feeling sad about it, he decided to do something bold: he started his own organization, "Lobby for Animals," to stand up for animals' rights.

Now, founding an organization isn't exactly something every 12-year-old does. But Thomas was determined. Lobby for Animals had a simple yet powerful mission: to make people aware of animal cruelty and encourage everyone to show compassion toward animals. And he wasn't just talking about it; he was ready to work hard to make a real difference.

Thomas became a passionate advocate, which means he spoke up for animals in a big way. He researched, wrote letters, spoke to officials, and even gave presentations to help people understand how they could help animals. For example, he talked about the importance of adopting pets from shelters instead of buying from breeders and pet stores that might not treat animals kindly. Thomas believed every animal deserved a safe, loving home and a happy life, and he wanted others to believe it, too.

One of Thomas's biggest goals was to help end practices that caused harm or suffering to animals. He believed that animals had feelings and deserved to be treated with respect and care. So he worked to stop things like animal testing and factory farming, where animals can be kept in small, uncomfortable spaces and treated like objects instead of living beings.

So, how did Thomas make a difference? By raising awareness and speaking directly to lawmakers. While most people his age might feel nervous about meeting with important people, Thomas was fearless. He would walk right into meetings, sit down with government officials, and tell them why it was important to protect animals. He didn't just give them his opinion—Thomas came prepared, armed with facts, research, and stories to help these adults see things from an animal's perspective. This dedication earned him a lot of respect, and many people started to listen to what he had to say.

Thomas also worked to inspire other kids and teens to get involved. He would give speeches at schools, write articles, and share his knowledge so that other young people would know they could make a difference, too. Thomas didn't just want to be the only kid helping animals; he wanted to create an entire generation of animal protectors who cared about kindness and compassion.

The coolest part? Thomas didn't come from a big city or a powerful family—he was just an ordinary kid who loved animals and wanted to help. His courage and determination show that you don't need to be an adult to make a big impact. All it takes is a big heart, a lot of passion, and the bravery to stand up for what's right.

With "Lobby for Animals," Thomas has proven that kids can change the world, one small step at a time. Whether it's convincing people to adopt a shelter pet, helping to stop animal testing, or simply spreading awareness about compassion, Thomas's work continues to inspire others to speak up for those who can't speak for themselves.

For Thomas, kindness meant taking action to protect the creatures he cared about most. And by doing so, he created a ripple effect that's helping animals all over the world live better, happier lives.

A KIND HEART SHINES BRIGHTEST!

CHAPTER 20:

A Heart Full of Kindness

At just four years old, Joshua Williams had a big heart and a big idea. While most kids were figuring out how to build the tallest Lego towers or color inside the lines, Joshua was already dreaming about something much bigger: helping people in need. One day, while riding in the car with his mom, Joshua noticed a homeless man on the side of the road holding a sign asking for food. Joshua's young mind couldn't shake the thought, "Why doesn't everyone have enough to eat?"

So, he did something extraordinary. Joshua took his birthday money—yep, the kind that usually goes to toys and treats—and used it to buy food. He made sandwiches, packed them with care, and gave them to people who needed a meal. That first act of kindness lit a spark inside Joshua. Seeing the smiles on people's faces when he handed them food made him feel like he was doing something truly important. And he was just getting started.

Joshua didn't stop with a few sandwiches. He wanted to help even more people, so he founded an organization called Joshua's Heart Foundation. He was only a kid, but he had a mission as big as his heart: to end hunger in his community and beyond. Now, starting a foundation might sound like a lot for a kid, but Joshua didn't let that hold him back. With the help of family, friends, and supporters, he got to work.

Joshua's Heart Foundation grew, and so did Joshua's impact. He and his team started organizing food drives, partnering with grocery stores, and collecting donations. Volunteers would fill boxes and bags with food, and Joshua would lead them in delivering meals to people who needed them most. Soon enough, Joshua's Heart Foundation was helping people in multiple communities, reaching hundreds, then thousands of people!

But Joshua didn't just want to give food; he wanted to help others in the fight against hunger. He spoke at schools, encouraging kids just like him to get involved. He showed them that even small acts of kindness—like donating a can of soup or giving a few minutes of their time—could make a huge difference. Soon, other kids were joining Joshua's Heart, packing bags, sorting food, and helping to deliver it to families in need.

Joshua also created a "Junior Advisory Board" so young people could have a voice in his foundation. Kids his age could help make decisions, organize events, and share ideas about how to fight hunger. Joshua believed that kids didn't have to wait until they were older to make a change. He wanted everyone to feel empowered to make a difference right now.

Since those first sandwich deliveries, Joshua's Heart Foundation has delivered over 2 million pounds of food to people in need. That's right, two million pounds! Imagine that much food stacked up—it's like feeding a city! All because one little boy believed he could help others.

What's even more inspiring? Joshua didn't do it for fame or rewards; he did it because he cared. His kindness and dedication inspired his family, friends, and even strangers to pitch in and help. Joshua showed the world that anyone can be a hero, no matter their age, as long as they have compassion and determination.

So, if you ever wonder if you're 'too young' to make a difference, think about Joshua. He started with one small act and turned it into a movement. Joshua's story shows that helping others can start with something as simple as sharing a meal—and that kindness has the power to create incredible change.

CONCLUSION

As you've read, kindness has the power to turn simple actions into something truly incredible. Each story in this book shows how young people—just like you—have used their compassion to make a real impact. These kids didn't need superpowers or magic. They started with a caring heart, a bit of courage, and a drive to help others, and look at what they accomplished!

Whether it's saving animals, protecting the environment, or bringing smiles to those in need, there's no limit to what kindness can achieve. And here's the best part: the power to do something amazing is already in your hands. Kindness is a gift you can give any day, anywhere, and it's a gift that grows each time you share it.

So, as you go forward, remember that every act of kindness—no matter how small—has the potential to make a big difference. Keep looking for ways to help, keep showing others you care, and let kindness be your superpower. Who knows what incredible things you'll do next? The world is waiting for a hero just like you.

Note from the Author

Dear Reader,

Thank you for joining me on this incredible journey. I hope you enjoyed the stories and learned something new along the way. Your feedback is incredibly valuable to me, and I would love to hear your thoughts.

If you enjoyed the book, please consider leaving a review on the Amazon page. Your review helps me improve and continue creating content that inspires and educates young minds.

Thank you for your support!

Best regards,

Made in United States
Orlando, FL
13 December 2024

55576921R00078